Prof. Toft's Zoo

Prof. Toff has a zoo keeper, Philip. They need to help the animals.

Jim has a chat with some animals.

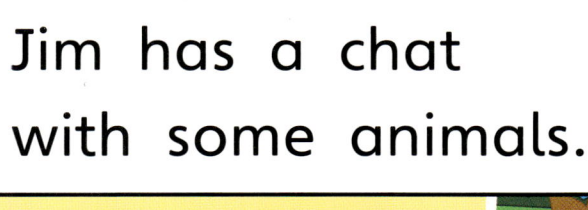

Oh! Boo!

They are all down in the dumps.

Hiss!

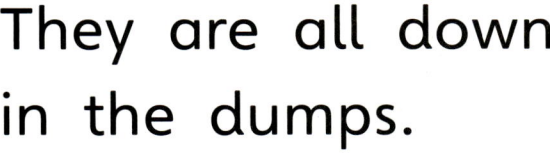

The animals think their zoo is too dull.

This is an alphabet trick.

a=1
b=2
c=3
d=4
e=5
f=6
g=7
h=8
i=9
j=10
k=11
l=12
m=13

n=14
o=15
p=16
q=17
r=18
s=19
t=20
u=21
v=22
w=23
x=24
y=25
z=26

8, 1, 22, 5   6, 21, 14

I think the elephant has got it!

What has Jim Vim got in the box?

Jim Vim lifts the lid off the box ...

Now the animals are sure that their zoo is the best!